Gliding Garter Snakes

by Buffy Silverman

Lerner Publications Company • Minneapolis

To Jeff, Jake, and Emma with love

Lerner Publications Company
A division of Lerner Publishing Group
241 First Avenue North
Minneapolis, MN 55401 U.S.A.

Website address: www.lernerbooks.com

Words in *italic* type are explained in a glossary on page 30.

Library of Congress Cataloging-in-Publication Data

Silverman, Buffy.
    Gliding garter snakes / by Buffy Silverman.
        p.   cm. — (Pull ahead books)
    ISBN-13: 978–0–8225–6043–2 (lib. bdg. : alk. paper)
    ISBN-10: 0–8225–6043–7 (lib. bdg. : alk. paper)
    1. Garter snakes—Juvenile literature. I. Title.
    II. Series.
    QL666.O636S55 2007
    597.96'2—dc22   2005024184

Manufactured in the United States of America
1 2 3 4 5 6 — JR — 12 11 10 09 08 07

A striped snake glides across the ground. What kind of snake is it?

It is a garter snake. Garter snakes
live near ponds and wetlands.
They live in forests and fields.

They can live in your backyard!

Garter snakes live where they find food. What do garter snakes eat?

Garter snakes are *carnivores*.
Carnivores eat other animals.

Garter snakes eat small animals such as earthworms, frogs, and fish.

The animals a garter snake hunts and eats are called its *prey*.

Garter snakes use their eyes to find
animals to eat.

Garter snakes also smell their prey.

A garter snake smells by flicking its tongue. Its tongue picks up scents from the air.

A frog is near! A garter snake grabs the frog and swallows it.

Some animals hunt garter snakes.

This hungry owl caught a snake.

How do garter snakes stay safe
when an enemy is near?

They hide under leaves or logs.

A garter snake's stripes can make it hard for an enemy to see it.

Count the stripes. Most garter snakes have three yellow stripes.

Garter snakes are *reptiles*.

Like other reptiles, a snake's skin is covered with *scales*.

Reptiles are *ectotherms*. Their bodies get colder if the air is cold.

This garter snake lies on a sunny rock to keep warm.

Where do garter snakes go when it is too cold for them outside?

They spend the winter underground. They curl together in a *den*.

When spring comes, the days grow
warm. Garter snakes leave their den.

In a few months, female garter snakes will be ready to have babies. Baby garter snakes grow inside their mother's body.

Late in summer, a female garter snake hides under leaves. There she gives birth to her babies.

A baby garter snake is born inside a clear pouch called a *birth sac*.

Soon each newborn snake breaks out of its birth sac.

Sometimes a mother garter snake stays with her babies. But she does not take care of them.

The little snakes care for themselves.

They crawl under logs and hide.

Young garter snakes find small animals to eat. They grow and grow.

What happens when a snake grows?

Its skin gets too tight.

The snake crawls out of its old skin. This is called shedding. It leaves its old skin behind.

The garter snake glides away. Where will it go?

Maybe it will look for worms in your backyard!

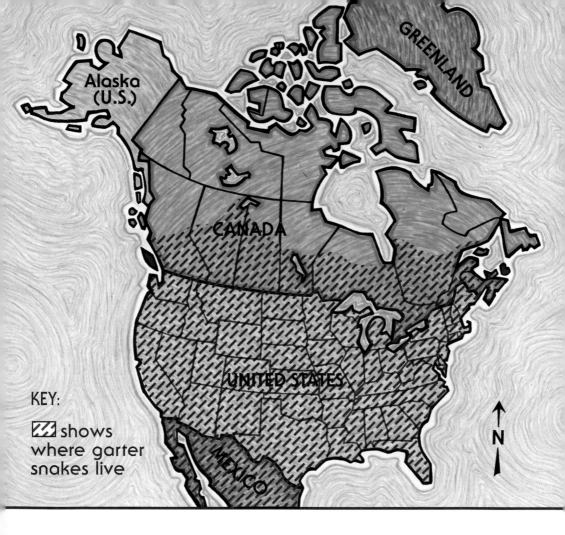

Alaska
(U.S.)

GREENLAND

CANADA

UNITED STATES

KEY:

▨ shows
where garter
snakes live

MEXICO

N

Find your state or province on this map.
Do garter snakes live near you?

Parts of a Garter Snake's Body

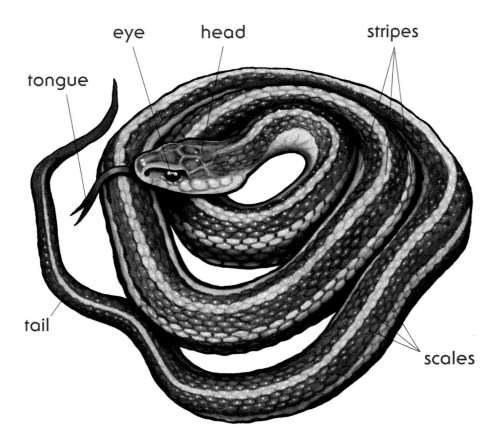

eye   head   stripes

tongue

tail

scales

Glossary

birth sac: a clear sac that covers a newborn garter snake

carnivores: animals that eat other animals

den: a cave or underground place where animals go to stay safe and warm

ectotherms: animals whose body temperature changes when the temperature of their surroundings changes

prey: animals that are hunted and eaten by other animals

reptiles: crawling or creeping animals that have scales. A reptile's body temperature changes when the temperature of its surroundings changes. Alligators, lizards, turtles, and snakes are reptiles.

scales: a tough, waterproof layer that covers and protects a reptile's skin

Further Reading and Websites

Lauber, Patricia. *Snakes Are Hunters*. New York: T. Y. Crowell, 1988.

Markle, Sandra. *Snakes: Biggest! Littlest!* Honesdale, PA: Boyds Mills Press, 2005.

Reptiles and Amphibians for Kids—Smithsonian National Zoological Park
http://nationalzoo.si.edu/Animals/RetilesAmphibians/ForKids/

Index

Photo Acknowledgments

The photographs in this book are reproduced through the courtesy of: © Dan Nedrelo, front cover, pp. 7, 12; © Allen Blake Sheldon, pp. 3, 5, 6, 8, 9, 10, 13, 14, 15, 17, 31; © Joe McDonald/TOM STACK & ASSOCIATES, INC., p. 4; © Joe McDonald/CORBIS, p. 11; © Francois Gohier/Photo Researchers, Inc., p. 16; © Alan Francis, pp. 18, 19, 20, 21, 23; © Jim Merli/Visuals Unlimited, p. 22; © Bill Beatty/Visuals Unlimited, p. 24; © Robert Folz/Visuals Unlimited, p. 25; © James E. Gerholdt, pp. 26, 27.